A YEAR OF ABUNDANCE

A YEAR OF
Abundance

DAILY PRACTICES AND AFFIRMATIONS TO CREATE JOY, GRATITUDE, AND CONNECTION

NORA DAY

ROCKRIDGE
PRESS

Series Designer: Alyssa Nassner
Interior and Cover Designer: Lisa Schreiber
Art Producer: Tom Hood
Editor: Adrian Potts
Production Editor: Andrew Yackira
Production Manager: Jose Olivera

Author photograph courtesy of Rozy Kay

ISBN: Print 978-1-64876-781-4 | eBook 978-1-63807-135-8

R0

For all the yogis, yoginis, meditators,
and abundant thinkers and doers;
I thank you for your sweet inspiration.

"Your most precious, valued possessions and your greatest powers are invisible and intangible. No one can take them. You, and you alone, can give them. You will receive abundance for your giving. The more you give—the more you will have!"

—W. CLEMENT STONE

Contents

Introduction

YOUR ABUNDANT LIFESTYLE—ONE THAT NOURISHES, BALANCES, and brings limitless happiness to all areas of your life—is waiting to surround you. Living an abundant lifestyle means tuning in to the beauty and blessings of the universe, and celebrating the quiet joys and simple pleasures of everyday life. It involves a practice of gratitude, self-care, and extending kindness to other beings and the planet. Abundance is not about creating more material goods or wealth; rather, it's about aligning yourself with the bounties of the universe so that you can step into your power and create your best life.

Embracing your abundant lifestyle doesn't require complicated training or expertise; it simply requires that you feel gratitude and compassion for yourself. But sometimes, figuring out just how to do that can seem challenging. *A Year of Abundance* is designed to help you feel that gratitude, align to your true purpose and passion, and connect with a daily mindset of abundance. In each of this book's daily entries, you will find an inspiring prompt, practice, reflection, exercise, or affirmation that will help you find creative ways to be grateful for what you have and achieve a more gratifying, nurturing, and loving lifestyle. Each entry will offer a new opportunity to experience and benefit from your abundance mindset.

You can start this program any day, not just on January 1st. When you start connecting with your appreciation, gratitude, and happiness for what you have, the universe steps in to align you to your dreams and desires. Fear and doubt fade away as self-acceptance and self-confidence begin to shine. Inviting abundance into your life is not a race or competition. Your limitless abundance is always working its way to you at your perfect pace.

For over 25 years, I have practiced yoga and meditation with an open heart, an open mind, and a core feeling of abundance. During this time, I have been able to manifest an abundant lifestyle and teach others how to do the same. I wrote this book to help you create your daily mindset of abundance. I truly believe that on this planet, there is more than enough to go around for everybody, as the universe's supply is endless.

My yoga and meditation practices have taught me about the importance of maintaining an abundance mindset as opposed to a scarcity mindset. A scarcity mindset, which focuses on feeling like you don't have enough, blocks the energy flow, preventing positive thinking, appreciation, and self-worth from flowing freely. Meanwhile, an abundance mindset—one that focuses on what you have instead of what you don't have—unlocks any blockages and allows appreciation and gratitude to flow with a natural ease and calm. Once you've embraced an abundance mindset, you'll also start to embrace an uncompetitive, greed-free attitude, which will create more space in your life for giving, receiving, and thriving.

While this book can help guide you on your journey of abundance, it's not a substitute for psychological treatment for mental health issues like depression or anxiety. If you're struggling with ongoing or debilitating worry or sadness, please seek care from a medical professional or therapist. There is no shame in asking for help.

Once you begin working with the practices in this book, the compassion and gratitude that you feel for yourself will increase, which will manifest into having, doing, and believing that you are worthy of all your desires. This book is here to guide you, with unwavering trust, gratitude, and self-love, to your life of never-ending abundance.

JANUARY

1

1

JANURY

....

YOU'VE GOT THIS

Right as you wake up, close your eyes and take three slow, deep breaths. As each breath calms your nervous system, remind yourself how abundant, confident, and ready you are to start your day.

2

JANUARY

....

AFFIRMATION FOR YOUR INNER VOICE

Loving-kindness starts with yourself. Put it into practice by saying this affirmation, either quietly or out loud:

"My self-talk is uplifting, complimentary, and confident."

3

JANUARY

·········

I'M HAPPY FOR YOU

When you are truly happy for someone else's success, your own success will flourish. There is enough for you and everyone else on the planet.

4

JANUARY

·········

GRATITUDE MOMENTS

Expand your mindset to allow for more gratitude. With your mind focused on gratitude, you will receive the peaceful clarity needed to appreciate all of the abundance in your life today.

Make a mental note throughout your day every time something makes you feel appreciative. It could be something as simple as the sun shining through your window, the soothing feeling of a warm blanket, or the comfort of drinking your favorite coffee or tea.

5

JANUARY
·········

RELEASING RESISTANCE

Don't be afraid to change and redirect your goals. As you release your resistance and fears, your abundance energy becomes fine-tuned to your purpose.

6

JANUARY
·········

YES MANTRAS

Today is your day to say "yes" mantras. Here are three mantras to repeat to yourself throughout your day.

1. Yes, I am worthy.
2. Yes, I am limitless.
3. Yes, I am appreciative.

7

·······

BODY AWARENESS

Move your body in your favorite physical exercise, and feel expansive appreci-ation and awareness of your body. You could practice yoga, go for a walk, play basketball, or dance—whatever makes you feel connected to yourself.

8

JANUARY
·······

R-E-S-P-E-C-T

Giving respect, self-love, and encouragement to yourself is the first step to abundant gratitude.

When you take care of yourself with positive words and uplifting emotions, you realize how much you have to be thankful for every single day. Treat your-self with loving-kindness to receive the respect you deserve.

9

JANURY
·······

GIVING HOLIDAY

Do you give to everyone else but forget to give anything to yourself? Claim this day as your personal giving holiday. You could take yourself to lunch, buy yourself a gift, or have a spa day. Today, give yourself the things that make you feel happy and thriving so that you can consistently be the beautiful, caring person that you are.

10

JANURY
·······

"The first step toward discarding a scarcity mentality involves giving thanks for everything that you have."

—WAYNE W. DYER

11

JANUARY

. . . .

TO WHOM IT MAY CONCERN

Find a quiet place in your home where you won't be disturbed for at least five minutes.

Write out five wishes for your inner spiritual guide. After you have written them down, silently feel the feeling of having each dream realized. No need to visualize them—simply imagine how it would feel to have your dreams come true. When you feel the feeling of your own abundance, you are aligning with your dreams.

12

JANUARY

. . . .

UNDIVIDED ATTENTION

You invite into your life whatever you give the most attention to. Experience endless ease and health as you give your undivided attention to your well-being.

13

JANUARY

....

I AM LOVED

When you saturate your thoughts with loving, uplifting thoughts, negative energy falls away. Recite this mantra to yourself throughout your day: "I am loved." This simple mantra nourishes the soul and keeps loving energy flowing.

14

JANUARY

....

CHANGING NATURE

Nature itself is not static; it is constantly changing. You are part of Mother Nature's domain; you, too, are always changing. Accept the constant changes of your life as a gift to grow into your life's purpose.

15

JANUARY

....

AFFIRMATION FOR GIFTING

Channel the bounties of the universe by repeating this mantra, either quietly or out loud:

"The universe gifts me with endless abundance at every possible turn."

16

JANUARY

....

BALANCING ACT

When your mind and body balance each other in a peaceful, quiet state, you achieve harmony. You can easily find your balanced state by sitting comfortably in a cross-legged position with your eyes closed and hands in your lap. Count 10 rounds of slow breaths. Allow your relaxing inhales and exhales to bring you balance.

17

JANUARY
· · · · · · · ·

LOVING RELATIONSHIPS

In order to share a fulfilling, abundant, loving relationship with your partner, give up jealousy, competition, and the need to always be right. In order to create a fulfilling, abundant, loving relationship with yourself, embrace treating yourself with forgiveness and kindness, and self-care rituals, like breathing exercises.

18

JANUARY
· · · · · · · ·

RANDOM ACTS OF KINDNESS

There are endless opportunities for you to perform random acts of kindness, today and every day. You could offer to babysit your nieces and nephews, walk your neighbor's dog, or cook a meal for a friend. Your limitless generosity gives you the power to uplift and inspire.

19

JANUARY

....

YOU ARE TAKEN CARE OF

Trust that you are exactly where you need to be, doing the exact right thing, at the perfect time in your life. You are completely taken care of.

20

JANUARY

....

BLESSED

As you lie down for bed, make a mental list of all the things that made you feel grateful today. You could be thankful for your healthy body, your job, or the unconditional love your pet gives you—anything that makes you feel happy, loved, or cared for counts. You are a blessed, unending source of gratitude.

21

JANUARY

....

"My good now flows to me in a steady, unbroken, ever-increasing stream of success, happiness and abundance."

—FLORENCE SCOVEL SHINN

22

JANUARY

....

FEARLESSNESS

When you believe that all things are possible, your fear fades away. Optimism helps you become a fearless master at manifesting abundance at every turn.

23

JANUARY
....

FRESH PERSPECTIVE

When you do the same thing over and over but can't seem to make any head-way on your goal, check in with your fresh perspective. Consider a new way to approach the same problem that might yield brand-new results. For example, if you can't seem to get into a full headstand at yoga class because fear is holding you back, take your headstand to the wall for a safe and comfortable space.

24

JANUARY
....

NOW HEAR THIS

Listen to your favorite song or piece of music to entice your senses, and let your spirit overflow with inspiration and beauty. Carry that feeling with you throughout the day.

25

JANUARY
·········

HEALING VISUALIZATION

You are a never-ending source of love, from top to bottom, side to side, front to back, inside and out. With your eyes closed, visualize your healing energy radiating outward into an expansive halo circling your entire body. Your healing energy is always watching over you.

26

JANUARY
·········

JOY

When you are in a state of great pleasure and happiness, you feel abundance. Surround yourself with joyful people to create a positive, emotional foundation.

27

JANUARY

· · · · · · · ·

BIRD'S-EYE VIEW

Imagine watching yourself from far above, with no worries, fears, or doubts.
When you change the viewfinder of your current situation, you see that you
have endless options and opportunities.

28

JANUARY

· · · · · · · ·

SELF-ASSURANCE

Trust, with unabashed confidence, that everything is working out for you every
day. There is only ceaseless self-assurance encircling you.

29

JANUARY
....

CORE BREATHING

Lie on your back with your palms on your stomach, near your navel, and your eyes closed. Feel the gentle rhythm of your inhale and exhale through the palms of your hands. As you do this, notice the miracle of your body's unlimited ability to breathe precious life into your being.

30

JANUARY
....

BIG BLUE SKY

The infinite, vast sky is as endless as your never-ending hope, joy, dreams, possibilities, and love.

31

TRUST

Everyone in the world, including you, can pluck their wishes from the infinite source of the universe. Your unfulfilled wishes become fulfilled when you fully trust there is enough for everyone.

FEBRUARY

19

1

FEBRUARY

. . . .

FEEL THE FEELS

When you intimately feel certainty, sureness, self-confidence, and steadiness, you are in the receiving mode for abundance.

2

FEBRUARY

. . . .

IMAGINATION ACTIVATION

Join a friend for a walk through your neighborhood, in a local park, or on your favorite trail. As you walk, toss around ideas about your perfect life. You could talk about the money you want to have, the place you want to live, the relationship or lifestyle you desire—let your imagination guide you. Talking about your abundant lifestyle brings it closer to reality.

3

FEBRUARY
········

AFFIRMATION FOR THRIVING

Part ways with a scarcity mindset by reciting this affirmation:
"I relinquish competing with others to make space to thrive on my own terms."

4

FEBRUARY
········

CONSISTENCY AND PATIENCE

You are always being guided down the right path in life. Consistency and patience will gracefully bring your prescribed abundance to you.

5

FEBRUARY

....

BREAKFAST MEDITATION

Eat your breakfast in silence and reserve this time as your morning meditation. Stay committed to your silence by making sure there are no interruptions—no phones, no computers, and no television. Allow gratitude for the silverware, plates, bowls, napkins, and food on your table. Indulge in absolute appreciation for your plentiful breakfast experience.

6

FEBRUARY

....

I DO

I promise to be true to myself in good times and in bad, in sickness and in health. I will always love and honor myself, all the days of my life.

7

FEBRUARY

·······

WELCOME ABUNDANCE

Fill your life with quality people. Meaningful relationships are a primary source of richness, connection, and acceptance. Host a potluck dinner and invite both old and new friends to your house for a meal as you welcome abundance into your home.

8

FEBRUARY

·······

"You are, at this moment, standing right in the middle of your own 'acres of diamonds.'"

—EARL NIGHTINGALE

9

FEBRUARY

········

CHEERLEADER

You are your own most enthusiastic supporter. Never let anyone else undermine your unequivocal winningness.

10

FEBRUARY

········

FAST TRACK

Do you ever feel like you are working hard at achieving an abundant lifestyle but aren't getting immediate results? Here are four mini-mantras to say, silently or out loud, throughout your day to get on the fast track to manifestation:

1. I am consistent.
2. I visualize the life I want.
3. I allow patience into my life.
4. I receive love with a sense of humbleness.

11

FEBRUARY

....

HEALTHY EQUALS WEALTHY

When you have a healthy mind, body, and soul, you are wealthy in every area of your life.

12

FEBRUARY

....

CLEAN ENERGY

Close your eyes, stand firm on the earth with your arms by your sides, and inhale deeply. Then, as you exhale, say a prolonged "HA" out loud. Repeat five times. The vibration of "HA" on the exhale eliminates stale energy from your body and mind, while the inhale replenishes you with clean energy.

13

FEBRUARY

....

BRAKE FOR ABUNDANCE

When you push so hard to achieve success, sometimes you can push it away. Hit the brakes to see the abundance right in front of you.

14

FEBRUARY

....

AFFIRMATION FOR LOVE

Embrace yourself as you are right now by reciting this affirmation:
"I embrace and love my ageless, authentic self."

15

FEBRUARY

....

THINK ABOUT IT

If you want to be a millionaire, think about your abundant bank account. If you want to have a loving relationship, think about how it might feel to walk around with your beloved partner. If you want to live on a tropical island, think about breathing the ocean air. Imagine yourself in the circumstances you want by thinking them to fruition.

16

FEBRUARY

....

TAKE A HINT

When positive coincidences keep appearing all around you, it's a hint of the prosperity coming your way soon.

17

....

COMPASSION AND FORGIVENESS

Can you think of a relative you haven't spoken to for a long time? Mend fences with family members by reaching out and setting compassion and forgiveness into motion. By taking action to enrich your family circle, you are inviting more possibilities of abundance into your life.

18

FEBRUARY

....

INTUITION

Does your inner voice alternate between a laid-back surfer and an aggressive boss? Find balance by listening to your intuition. Trust your instincts for ever-lasting success.

19

FEBRUARY

....

ORDER UP

Giving back to your community creates a sense of belonging and enhances your family and work values. Dine at a local restaurant or café, donate to a local charity, start a food drive in your neighborhood, or simply buy something from a nearby small business.

20

FEBRUARY

....

TEACH ME

When you practice what you teach, you immerse yourself in the ultimate truth of your knowledge and in return receive unlimited gratification.

21

FEBRUARY

· · · · · · · ·

"Your crown has been bought and paid for. Put it on your head and wear it."

—DR. MAYA ANGELOU

22

FEBRUARY

· · · · · · · ·

SOUNDING BOARD

Make a list of three people who empower you, give you courage, move you forward, and make you feel more confident. These people are your sounding board for trusted ideas and opinions to further your absolute success.

23
FEBRUARY
·········

EMPATHY

Allow empathy into your life through your consistent attention to loving-kindness.

24
FEBRUARY
·········

WORD GAME

Pick an uplifting, inspiring "word of the day" for yourself today, like *grace* or *joy*. Keep this word in your subconscious mind, and write it down or say it out loud throughout the day—at the gym, at work, at home, or while having a meal. Witness the power of the word to influence your daily abundance.

25

FEBRUARY

....

TAKE TIME TO ORGANIZE

Over your morning tea, smoothie, coffee, or juice, have a notepad or device handy. With a clear mind, write down your daily schedule, and include ways to make your day more joyful. You could book a private training session, make dinner plans with a colleague you want to share ideas with, or take yourself out to a movie. Take time to organize, so that you can feel more abundant and clear-headed for your day.

26

FEBRUARY

....

HONEST MOMENTS

Make yourself a cup of hot cocoa or tea to relax and unwind as you take an honest moment to reflect on the good, the challenging, and the ambitious parts of your life. By giving yourself this calming time, you can clearly move forward in the right direction on your life's path.

27

FEBRUARY
·········

VALUABLE UNIQUENESS

Instead of focusing your attention on feelings of unworthiness, reposition your focus on your valuable uniqueness. Have the courage and confidence to believe in yourself.

28

FEBRUARY
·········

LEAVE IT BEHIND

As you leave behind your past, close your eyes and visualize walking through a tropical forest filled with colorful foliage, abundant fruit trees, and majestic waterfalls. Let your mental picture of the overflowing forest remind you that today and every day, there is more than plenty of everything for everyone.

29

FEBRUARY

....

WAITING IN LINE

Endless opportunities are waiting in line to enchant and delight you.

MARCH

MARCH

·········

RAISE YOUR VIBRATION

List your positive emotional characteristics out loud or in your head. You could say something like, "I love my attitude of gratitude, I love being happy, and I love being eager and excited for my day." Say at least three (but try for as many as you can think of) to raise your vibration for a continual positive attitude.

MARCH

·········

SMILE

Share your kindness, happiness, and bright outlook by freely giving smiles to others.

3

MARCH
....

ME DAY

Make an appointment with yourself to take a bubble bath, get a massage, go to a movie, or enjoy any other pampering activity. When you take care of yourself, you are forever taken care of.

4

MARCH
....

AN ODE TO THE SUN

As the sun shines on the whole world, it ripens the fruits of the earth and gives light and warmth to all living beings. Take a moment to give thanks for the endless nourishment the sun gives every day.

5

MARCH
....

"A flower does not think of competing with the flower next to it. It just blooms."

—SENSEI OGUI

6

MARCH
....

SLEEPY TIME

When you get a good night's sleep, you feel refreshed, calm, and confident. These feelings bring limitless fresh ideas and optimism to your day. Here are a few sleepy-time tips:

1. Drink plenty of water during the day so you are properly hydrated at bedtime.
2. Avoid caffeine after 8 p.m.
3. Put your phone on silent mode before you go to sleep.
4. Silently count to 10, over and over, to lull yourself to sleep.

7

MARCH
....

VOLUNTEER

When you are generous with your time, you create an abundance mindset. Volunteering is a wonderful way to give without expecting anything in return.

8

MARCH
....

EMOTIONAL ATTRACTION

With your eyes closed, visualize your perfect place to live. Envision the climate, the country, the mountains or ocean nearby, the language spoken by your neighbors, the food served in the local café; be as specific as possible. For the next few minutes, sit quietly and believe that you are living there now. Emotionally attract your new home with infinite confidence.

9

MARCH

....

LOST AND FOUND

You can't lose your abundance. It is ever present, as long as there is patience and an unwavering attention to gratitude.

10

MARCH

....

AFFIRMATION FOR OPPORTUNITIES

Expand your horizons by saying this affirmation:

"My challenges are opportunities to gain a broader view for positive change."

11

....

BODY LANGUAGE

To exude a calm confidence inside and out, try this pose: Broaden your shoulders, lengthen your torso, and stand firmly on the ground. This stance telegraphs comfortable strength, ease, and assuredness. Strike this pose to give your inner self a continual confidence boost while also exuding a trusting presence.

12

MARCH

....

THE NEW CURRENCY

Your proactive mindset is your new currency. Give yourself permission to wish, dream, and visualize your limitless potential.

13

MARCH
....

HEALTH GOALS

You make your best decisions when you are healthy, alert, and vibrant. Here are some ways to get in mental and physical shape for your abundant lifestyle:

1. Take a brisk 30-minute walk three to six times a week.
2. Meditate for 15 minutes daily.
3. Journal uplifting mantras and affirmations every day.
4. Practice yoga three to six times a week.

14

MARCH
....

EMOTION POTION

Happiness, gratitude, and eagerness are your emotional potions for ceaseless success.

15

MARCH
·········

TAKE THE INITIATIVE

To bring a sense of optimism and hope to your desires, take the initiative. If you want a new car, go test-drive the model you want. If you are looking for a romantic relationship, subscribe to a dating site. If you want to go on vacation, schedule an appointment with a travel agent. When you take the initiative to fulfill your desires, you open up endless possibilities.

16

MARCH
·········

"I am unlimited in my own ability to create the good in my life."

—LOUISE HAY

17
MARCH
········

HIGH SPIRITS

Personal worth begins in the mind. Keep your spirits high with these mantras about self-appreciation and self-respect:
"I love myself. I am worth it. I am beautiful."

18
MARCH
········

BAREFOOT

Take your shoes off at the park, on the beach, or anywhere you can connect with nature below your bare feet. "Earthing" or "grounding" works when your body is in direct contact with the earth, making an electrical connection with its energies. Walk slowly and gently, letting the awe-inspiring and infinite energy of Mother Nature completely fill your soul.

19

MARCH

....

ABUNDANCE CONSCIOUSNESS

When you believe there is plenty of everything, even if it isn't part of your life today, your existence flows with balanced ease.

20

MARCH

....

PEACE OUT

To increase your peaceful abundance, make time for more self-reflective activities. You could schedule a private yoga class, practice tai chi in the park, get a massage, or go for a silent sunrise beach walk. The more tranquility and peace you instill in your mind and body, the more balanced and aligned with abundance you become.

21

MARCH
·········

JOYFUL ENERGY

Keep your energy flowing toward joy. Joyful energy gives you life, energy, and power.

22

MARCH
·········

ENDLESS HOPE

When you feel sad or unmotivated, close your eyes and visualize yourself in your favorite place. You could imagine having a chocolate croissant at a café in Paris, sailing in Saint-Tropez, or playing in the gentle waves in Hawaii. Soften your mind by imagining happy experiences that bring endless hope.

23

MARCH

....

ABUNDANTLY INFUSED

Ramp up your healthy diet for a clearer mind and more agile body. Set yourself up for success by consuming more plant-based foods that are infused with the life force and abundance of nature.

24

MARCH

....

MAKE THE SHIFT

Start shifting your thoughts and behaviors by focusing on one attribute you want more of in your life. You could focus on increasing self-confidence, self-worth, inspiration, cheerfulness, or optimism. Let whichever one you choose saturate your being in never-ending supplies.

25
MARCH
....

AFFIRMATION FOR LETTING GO

Offer yourself loving-kindness by reciting this affirmation:
"As I let go of unworthiness, acceptance and self-love permeate my thoughts."

26
MARCH
....

MAGICAL NATURE

Spending time in nature is a reminder of the massive abundance that surrounds you at all times, from the birds and butterflies to the sunshine, rain, and even snow. Let nature show you the true meaning of magical abundance.

27
MARCH
....

AHA MOMENT

Have you ever had a moment when a friend's words or a passage from a book sparked a great idea? Instead of waiting for that aha moment, start planting your own seeds of opportunity. Write down as many ideas as you can think of—for a new business, an invention, a unique lifestyle, or anything else that can kick-start your aha moment.

28
MARCH
....

SHOW UP FOR GRATITUDE

When you show up for gratitude, you are showing up for self-worth, self-confidence, and self-love.

29

MARCH

....

CONTENTMENT

Sit quietly with your eyes closed and your hands in your lap. Visualize that there is abundance, on every level, for every person in the world. There is no competition. You are not competing with anyone for anything, because you and everyone else have more than enough. Sit for five minutes with this feeling of profound contentment washing over you.

30

MARCH

....

PART OF PLENTY

You are infinitely capable of creating new things. You are part of what the universe is constantly creating.

31

....

AUTHENTICALLY YOU

Take a walk in your neighborhood. Walk in silence and reflect on what makes you authentically you. It could be your daily commitment to your well-being, your generous nature, your fearless ability to try new things—anything that gives you a continuous sense of pride and self-respect in being completely yourself.

APRIL

1

APRIL

....

DIRECT LINK

Your emotional self-love is directly linked to your physical acceptance. You have ample self-love, inside and out.

2

APRIL

....

BEAUTIFUL LIFESTYLE

To attract your beautiful lifestyle, view challenges as opportunities to thrive rather than feeling that you have already failed because things aren't going perfectly. Slow down enough to give undivided attention to your work, your well-being, and your friends and family. Allow your beliefs to move you forward instead of holding you back. Rather than making excuses for your mistakes, own them, and have faith that something better will happen because of them.

3

APRIL
....

"Abundance is the quality of life you live and the quality of life you give others."

—J. K. ROWLING

4

APRIL
....

GIVE AND FORGIVE

To truly give and forgive, overcome negative feelings. Pick someone in your life whom you've held a grudge against, or haven't spoken to in a long time because of negativity. Muster up the courage to contact them, and begin your nonstop path of forgiveness.

5

APRIL
....

GREEDLESS

The easiest way to receive and create new opportunities is through a selfless mindset. When you are not greedy, and instead give and serve, you receive abundance at a much faster rate, because you are not taking more than your share. Instead, you are gaining more than you ever imagined.

6

APRIL
....

EXPANSIVE MINDSET

Look up at the sky and notice the infinity that surrounds you. Close your eyes and visualize what direction your life can take with no boundaries, no limits, no end in sight. Live in this expansive mindset today.

7

APRIL
....

CONSTANT OVERFLOW

Being abundant means experiencing a constant overflow—what you need is constantly coming to you, now and in the future.

8

APRIL
....

A SLOWER PACE

In your fast-paced life, make time to practice the exact lifestyle you want to live each day. Focus on slowing down. You could eat a meal slowly to enjoy each bite, take time to notice the shapes of clouds, or luxuriate in the warming comfort of a longer shower or bath. When you make more time for abundance, you receive more abundance.

9

APRIL
·········

COMING OF AGE

You are an ageless being whose mental and physical characteristics are eternally youthful.

10

APRIL
·········

THE UNIMAGINABLE BECOMES IMAGINABLE

Without timidity or doubt, envision the unimaginable as imaginable. Write down five ways your life could be flooded with never-ending abundance. You could be with the love of your life, live in your favorite city, have beautiful children, or work at your dream job. In your mind's eye, have complete confidence in your power to create.

11

APRIL

. . . .

AFFIRMATION FOR PROSPERITY

Manifest success with this affirmation:

"Prosperity surrounds me on a higher level than it ever has before."

12

APRIL

. . . .

CHOOSE RIGHT

Today, choose to be in the right place with the right work, right wealth, right health, and right love. Surround yourself with what makes you feel good, happy, and worthy to attract more abundance into your life.

13

APRIL
....

POISED

When you are self-aware, you are ready to adapt. No matter what you are faced with, maintain a poised demeanor and adjust.

14

APRIL
....

GARDENING FOR PEACE

It is such a great gift to plant your own food, flowers, and other greenery and watch the magnificence of Mother Nature bloom. If you don't have a back-yard or front yard where you could start a garden, plant with garden pots on a windowsill. As you relax into the repetition of working with the soil, allow your gardening to become your peaceful meditation.

15

APRIL

·········

INVISIBLE CONTRACT

Sign an invisible contract signifying your everlasting commitment to prioritizing your health and well-being.

16

APRIL

·········

EMPOWERED

When you take full responsibility and acceptance of your feelings, you become forever empowered. Today, focus on one uplifting feeling you would like to feel permeating your soul. It could be happiness, eagerness, creativity, or any other positive emotion. Whether you are at home, at work, with friends, or exercising, feel this feeling with your mind and body for unending empowerment.

17
APRIL
......

"Abundance is about being rich,
with or without money."

—SUZE ORMAN

18
APRIL
......

CREDIT YOUR ACCOUNT

Think of physical exercise, like yoga, Pilates, running, tennis, or any other activity, as credits to your health account, which increase your abundant overall wealth.

19

APRIL
. . . .

TO-DO LIST

1. Let go of perfection
2. Let go of competition
3. Let go of jealousy
4. Let go of hate
5. Let go of fear

20

APRIL
. . . .

WHAT GOES AROUND COMES AROUND

Paying constant attention to your immeasurable self-worth brings a sense of humbled self-respect.

21
APRIL
·········

FREEDOM MANTRA

Repeat this mantra today to remind yourself of your ability to choose:
"Today, I choose to be a free thinker of positive, creative, uplifting thoughts."

22
APRIL
·········

HOME SWEET HOME

Fill your home with reminders of abundance, like pictures that foster gratitude and appreciation. You could hang pictures of beautiful, expansive landscapes that represent never-ending beauty. Mother-and-baby pictures of your favorite animals bring enormous gratitude and help instill the idea of giving with no expectations. Let your home's sweet reminders of gratitude and appreciation overlap into your life.

23

....

AFFIRMATION FOR GOODNESS

Welcome goodness into your life with this affirmation:

"The law of attraction brings goodness to me from everyone and everywhere."

24

APRIL

....

SOUL HEALTH

Restore your well-being by unplugging for the day. Turn your devices off for a restorative day to enhance continual soul health.

25

·········

YOU DO YOU

No matter how others perceive you, in your core essence, you will always be you. Throughout your day, write down and keep a checklist of all of your authentic choices, whether they're related to food, work, love, or anything else. Write a sentence or two about how each choice positively affects your life goals. This writing exercise will bring you never-ending self-confidence and self-trust.

26

APRIL

·········

WHEN I GROW UP . . .

What do you want to be when you grow up? Each day, you can answer this question from your current spot on your perpetual life journey. Be patient, compassionate, and loving to yourself in order to become what you want to be.

27

APRIL

· · · · · · · ·

TWO STEPS CLOSER

There are millions of careers in the world, from actor to pilot to real estate agent. Take the first step and allow yourself to imagine working at your dream job. Then, take the second step and get more information about how to get there. Brush up your résumé. Making the leap between thinking about your dream job and taking the steps to make it happen reinstates your unwavering determination and steadfast commitment.

28

APRIL

· · · · · · · ·

PRETTY PLEASE

You strengthen the everlasting bond of "ask and you shall receive" through kindness, humility, "please," and "thank you."

29
APRIL
....

BOUNDLESS ENERGY

Stand with your hands on your hips, your feet shoulder-width apart, and your toes pointing forward. On your inhale, bend your knees and reach your arms up to the sky. On your exhale, straighten your legs and bring your hands back to your hips. Repeat 10 times, and feel the breath and movement give your mind and body boundless energy.

30
APRIL
....

LOVE AND DEVOTION

There is an infinite amount of love and devotion for you to give to yourself.

MAY

1

MAY

....

SHINE BRIGHT

Your aura is shining bright with all the never-ending new ideas percolating inside of you.

2

MAY

....

LIKE-MINDED

Write down three specific times when you surrounded yourself with like-minded people and had a positive result. It could be a successful professional project you did with coworkers, a romantic relationship that accelerated to a positive outcome, or any other experience you can think of. Your ability to recognize the long-term benefits of being near like-minded people contributes to your abundance mentality.

3
MAY
·········

UNKNOWN WORDS

The words in your heart's center are *authentic, caring, aware, honest,* and *mindful. Fake, jealous, egotistical,* and *pretentious* are unknown there.

4
MAY
·········

SPIRITUAL JOURNEY

Nurture your spiritual growth by feeding your soul with unconditional self-acceptance. Visualize your true self with patience, tolerance, forgiveness, or anything that brings continuous forward movement on your spiritual journey.

5

MAY
....

"The universe is not outside of you. Look inside yourself; everything that you want, you already are."

—RUMI

6

MAY
....

CUP HALF FULL

Whether you see your life as successful depends on whether you see your cup as half full or half empty. You have the continuous ability to fine-tune that focus.

7

MAY

....

BABY STEPS

In your mind's eye, envision your biggest dream. Then, make a small effort daily to get yourself there. You could make tangible changes to your life in order to get closer to making your dream a reality, or you could mentally commit through a meditation practice in which you visualize your dream coming closer. Either way, consistently take baby steps to unveil your destiny.

8

MAY

....

PATIENCE

When you push yourself to do something you are not ready to do, you become unbalanced. Manifest your potential steadily and patiently to achieve balance.

9
MAY
....

AROMATHERAPY

At bedtime, give yourself a personal aromatherapy session as you slip under the covers. Put a few drops of lavender or jasmine essential oil on your pillow to induce sleep and relaxation. Tension and stress will surrender as you sleep with lasting calm.

10
MAY
....

THANK YOU

Give thanks for the gentleness of the sunset, the ease of the sunrise, and the eternal acceptance of the time in between.

11

MAY
....

AFFIRMATION FOR INTERNAL DIALOGUE

Our thoughts are the source of our emotions and mood. Shake off your inner critic by saying this affirmation:

"My consistent and affirming internal dialogue is creating and inspiring my choices with every thought."

12

MAY
....

FEELING BLUE

Blue is associated with tranquility and calmness. To bring more peaceful vibes into your home and create an abundantly calming atmosphere, you could paint a blue sky on your ceiling, use a blue toothbrush, sleep on blue sheets, hang blue lights on your porch, or add any other blue adornments.

13
MAY
....

PUT ON YOUR GLASSES

For a clearer vision of your true passion and purpose, pay attention to the times you have been unequivocally happy. Those are the times you were aligned with your greater good.

14
MAY
....

BURNING ENTHUSIASM

In yoga, *tapas* is a word that means dedication, zest, and burning enthusiasm for yoga and life in general. To bring more tapas to your life, fill your day with fun, excitement, smiles, laughs, good food, and good friends. Let your burning enthusiasm know no boundaries.

15

MAY

....

"Life is a field of unlimited possibilities."

—DEEPAK CHOPRA

16

MAY

....

CONFIDENCE

Have confidence in your life choices by listening rather than reacting, receiving rather than pushing, and being grateful instead of resentful.

17

MAY
·········

SING A SONG

Singing is a great way to relieve anxiety, get your body pleasantly vibrating, and remember to not take yourself so seriously. You don't have to be a professional-level singer for this to work—just sing a favorite song and allow your vocalizing to bring sensations of endless freedom, hope, and joy to your heart.

18

MAY
·········

CHANGE THE NARRATIVE

You are here to experience love and happiness. Change the narrative in your subconscious mind from "I'm unhappy and unloved" to "I am happy; I am loved."

19
MAY
....

TIMELESS OCEAN

The ocean doesn't worry that it isn't getting enough waves made each day or about how perfect each wave is. Instead, it moves timelessly. In order to become more present in the moment, imagine yourself as the ocean, with its ebb and flow of waves that are not perfect, not rushing, but always moving toward their ideal destiny.

20
MAY
....

LOOK IN THE MIRROR

Every morning is a new day to look in the mirror, give yourself a sweet smile of humble self-confidence, and be overjoyed by the fresh abundance you are going to create in your day.

21

MAY
········

YOUR REAL SELF-WORTH

Your popularity or status on social media has nothing to do with your true self-worth. Take a day off from scrolling and posting, and instead, write down a paragraph or two about what you think determines your real self-worth. When you believe you are worthy and valuable, you are. You don't need "likes" to confirm or deny your innate self-worth.

22

MAY
········

GIVING GENEROUSLY

You can make this world a better, more abundant place by becoming an over-achiever at giving unselfishly.

23

MAY

....

SPEAK YOUR TRUTH

Use your phone or computer to record a video of yourself talking about your abundance mindset. It can be any length, as long as you say what you truly believe. You could speak about the power of visualization, the importance of self-care, the necessity of embracing change, or anything else that brings you closer to your abundance mindset. When you watch your video, know that the universe is also watching, listening, and abundantly providing.

24

MAY

....

AFFIRMATION FOR OPENHEARTEDNESS

Release judgment by reciting this mantra:
"I let go of old judgments and openheartedly embrace my new mindset of hope, gratitude, and trust."

25
MAY
....

UNCONDITIONAL LOVE

Admire, with no limitations, your courage, bravery, and self-love. All living beings benefit from your unconditional love.

26
MAY
....

ABUNDANCE QUESTIONS

Write out answers to each of these questions in order to gain clarity about your journey toward abundance.

1. What steps can I take to become more consistent in manifesting my dreams?
2. What are my go-to mantras or sayings that instill positive energy?
3. Who are the most encouraging and supportive people in my life and why?

27
MAY
....

VIBRATIONAL HAPPENINGS

When you think your efforts have gone unnoticed, always remember that most of what's happening is happening vibrationally. Infinitely trust the process.

28
MAY
....

GIVE YOURSELF THE GIFT OF SILENCE

On those days when you feel rejected, unnoticed, and unappreciated, give yourself a few minutes of silence. Sit quietly with your eyes closed, take slow, deep breaths, and wipe your mental slate clean. Generously give yourself uninterrupted silence.

29
MAY
. . . .

THE LAW OF PREPARATION

Prepare yourself for the never-ending gifts that are coming to you by emotionally and physically feeling that you already have them.

30
MAY
. . . .

SELFLESS SERVICE

Karma yoga is a style of yoga that focuses on selfless service and giving back to the community, with no expectation of getting credit. Pick an activity that will help you selflessly give back, like volunteering at a school, reading books or letters to a person who is visually impaired, or volunteering at a soup kitchen. Cultivate a sincere union between your abundant, giving actions and your community.

31

········

SPRING CLEANING

Cleanse harmful words and toxic thinking from your thoughts by focusing on self-love, self-care, and self-gratitude.

JUNE

1

JUNE
·········

PLENTITUDE OF LOVE

Today, you are abundantly loved, valued, honored, and appreciated by everyone you come into contact with. Bask in the plentitude of love that you are awash in.

2

JUNE
·········

PROS AND CONS

Write down the pros and cons of your job. Be completely honest about the gratifying aspects and the conflicts. You can write about things like your relationship with your boss, the hours you put in each day, the location, or anything else you can point out about your current work situation. Let your list be the guide to what the right or not-so-right job looks like for you.

3

JUNE
....

VISIONARY MINDSET

You truly have limitless possibilities. When you demonstrate fearless change and growth, you adopt a visionary mindset, which fuels your life's energy and passion.

4

JUNE
....

"The art of listening comes from a quiet mind and an open heart."

—RAM DASS

5

JUNE

....

WHAT MAKES YOU THANKFUL?

Today, observe what makes you thankful. It could be as simple as your shelter, your food, or the clothes on your back. The more observant and aware you are of the abundance you already have, the more consistently you'll feel gratitude in your heart.

6

JUNE

....

THE MIRACLE OF BREATHING

In the daytime, you breathe through your waking hours, and all night, you breathe peacefully through your sleep. Give thanks to the miracle of your breathing.

7

JUNE

....

SELF-CONFIDENCE LIST

To maintain self-confidence throughout your day, here are a few pointers:

- Accept and trust your skills with an attitude of honest clarity.
- Express your feelings directly and with respect.
- Treat yourself with compassion, no matter the outcome.

8

JUNE

....

ANXIETY BE GONE

Rather than living anxiously in the unknown future, stay present in the moment by becoming aware of the unlimited expanse of happiness right now.

9
JUNE
....

TURN THE VOLUME DOWN

When you are respectful to others, you are likely to be treated with respect by them. Today, consistently practice softening the volume of your voice. Speaking loudly can sometimes be seen as overbearing, showy, or rude, even if it isn't intended that way. Turn the volume down for good manners as abundant respect comes flowing to you.

10
JUNE
....

AFFIRMATION FOR MEDITATION

Welcome tranquility with this affirmation:
"Everlasting calm and peace surround me through my daily meditation."

11

JUNE
....

SAVOR THE PLEASURES

Eating slowly isn't just about ease of digestion; it's a practice focused on taking the time to savor the pleasures of food and nourishment. Paying attention to the pace at which you eat is a great mindfulness exercise. Today, practice eating your meals slowly to promote a less stressful life.

12

JUNE
....

DISAPPOINTMENT IS TEMPORARY

When you feel disappointed, remember: it's temporary. Use your unending patience and grace to visualize thoughts and emotions that satisfy your hopes and dreams.

13

JUNE

....

NEWNESS

Refresh your creativity with something new. It could be as simple as walking a different path to work, driving a different way home, getting coffee at a new coffee shop, or saying hello to someone you've seen before at the park, the gym, or the beach but have never previously spoken to. If you keep your outlook fresh, it will bring new ways of thinking and looking at things into your life.

14

JUNE

....

MAXIMUM QUALITY

Instead of prioritizing maximum quantity, align yourself to maximum quality. You are attracting long-term benefits and the characteristics of generous self-awareness and self-knowledge.

15

HIGH-IMPACT LIFE

To live a high-impact life full of passion and purpose, follow these steps:

- Do what you love, and the universe provides the path.
- Trust your intuition is guiding you to your purpose in life.
- Authentically engage your mind, body, and soul with your passion.
- Instead of disallowing and denying, fearlessly allow and receive.

16

JUNE
....

FORECAST

Rainy days clean the air, water, trees, and flowers and bring freshness to Mother Earth. Let the rain wash away your fears and doubts with a fresh forecast of hope and promise.

17
JUNE
·········

MOTIVATION LISTS

Here are some ideas to get you motivated for a healthy mind and body.

- Write down five healthy mind motivators, like a spiritual advisor session, an online guided meditation series, or anything else that would uplift your mindset.
- Write down five healthy body motivators, like a week with a personal trainer or hiking with a group to build supportive body awareness.
- Let your motivation lists urge you to take action for endless body and mind health.

18
JUNE
·········

BEAUTIFUL SELF

You are the first-made, original version of you—the master copy. Love, appreciate, and always adore your eternally unique, beautiful self.

19

JUNE

·······

"Develop enough courage so that you can stand up for yourself and then stand up for somebody else."

—DR. MAYA ANGELOU

20

JUNE

·······

15 MINUTES OF PEACE AND TRANQUILITY

Set a timer for 15 minutes and sit in a comfortable position with your eyes closed. Breathe in and out with a gentle smile on your lips, and allow everything in your life to be put on hold. Feel the abundant gratification of peace and tranquility.

21
JUNE
....

SELF-ADMIRATION

Give yourself heartfelt self-admiration for all of the abundance you continually create in your life.

22
JUNE
....

SHHH . . .

Pick three hours in the morning, afternoon, or evening to refrain from speaking. Unclutter your thoughts by excluding television, radio, social media, or any other distractions from your day. Instead, write down any thoughts, feelings, or ideas that arise from your quiet state. Silence makes space for mindful living by deliberately listening to your body and mind to cultivate a healthy way of being.

23
JUNE
·········

MAGICALLY MANIFESTING

What you dream about, think about, and focus on is magically manifesting on your behalf right now.

24
JUNE
·········

CHANGE OF SEASONS

Delight in the long days of summer. Take a walk while the sun is setting, go for an evening swim in the warm night air, or share a nighttime picnic. Allow the changes of the seasons to keep you forever flexible and able to adjust to different conditions.

25
JUNE

·······

PRACTICE

By consistently practicing self-respect and self-love toward yourself, your kind attitude allows overflowing abundance into your life.

26
JUNE

·······

PRESENT-MOMENT LIVING

The space between wanting something yesterday and patiently waiting for it is present-moment living. Believe that all things are coming at the exact time you are ready to receive them.

27
JUNE
....

PLANET LOVE

Pick up litter when you see it, avoid using plastics, and recycle regularly. Making consistent, positive progress to take care of the planet helps cultivate a sense of contribution to the greater good and self-appreciation.

28
JUNE
....

AFFIRMATION ON LOVE AT FIRST SIGHT

It's said that how you love yourself is how you teach others to love you. Say this affirmation and put its message into practice:

"I am devoted to my smiling face in the mirror. It's like love at first sight every day."

29
JUNE
....

EMOTIONS

Dance, music, and theater create a wide range of emotions, from sadness to joy. Appreciate that it is a gift to experience feelings on such an intimate level.

30
JUNE
....

GREET YOUR DAY

Before you start your morning routine, begin your day with a few things that bring you gratitude every morning. You could be thankful for your peaceful night's sleep, the strong legs that support your body, or your heart that beats healthily. Make it a habit to greet your day with appreciation and unwavering gratitude.

JULY

1

JULY

....

SENSORY PERCEPTION

Explore your world through your senses by observing the details of your environment. Notice the shape of a flower, the softness of its petals, its heady scent, or the texture of its leaves. When you are fully engaged in sensory perception, you are drawn completely into the moment and released from your mental chatter.

2

JULY

....

FULLY LIVING

Time wasted mentally rearranging your past choices could be time gained fully living your present choices.

JULY

········

OPEN-MINDEDNESS

As you practice open-mindedness, you practice being respectful of other people's opinions.

JULY

········

PEACE OF MIND

You create peace of mind by consistently synchronizing your thoughts with your ever-growing calm disposition. Today, vow not to get needlessly frustrated, agitated, or angry all day. Choose inner peace as your go-to reaction, over and over, so that you can thrive at your optimal level.

5

JULY

....

IMAGINATION WORKSHOP

Your imagination is your workshop to field ideas and research questions. Your imagination workshop transforms ideas into gratifying realities.

6

JULY

....

ASK FOR GUIDANCE

There is no shame in asking for help. When you are at a crossroads in your relationship, your work, or your spiritual learning, ask for guidance. Ask a friend, a professional, or a counselor to help you find the clarity you are looking for. Asking for guidance builds immeasurable personal trust and self-worth.

7

JULY
....

"The key to abundance is meeting limited circumstances with unlimited thoughts."

—MARIANNE WILLIAMSON

8

JULY
....

THINKING, SPEAKING, ACTING

When you think an uplifting thought, you can speak it. When you speak an uplifting thought, you can act upon it. When you act on your uplifting thought, you realize it.

9
JULY
....

ENDORPHINS

When you go outside and take a brisk walk or hike, you produce endorphins that trigger a positive feeling in your body, delivering an energizing outlook on life. To stay in optimal physical and mental health, go for regular walks or hikes, or join a group exercise class with your partner or a friend to get maximum support on your journey.

10
JULY
....

STEP INTO YOUR POWER

You are worth it! Step into your power through relentless thoughts of love and appreciation of your amazing, authentic self.

11

JULY

·······

RENEWED ENERGY

Give yourself one minute to take a few deep breaths and renew your energy. As you breathe, allow silence and clarity into your mind. As you use breathwork to pause your inner voice, you will naturally feel a sense of renewed energy.

12

JULY

·······

WELLNESS FOUNDATION

Build your wellness foundation from the ground up by adding more fruits and vegetables to your diet, exercising, meditating, and giving yourself daily self-love.

13
JULY
·······

AFFIRMATION FOR IMPERFECTIONS

Embrace your perfectly imperfect self by saying this affirmation whenever you need to:

"My beautiful imperfections make me forever me."

14
JULY
·······

TIME IS ON YOUR SIDE

Believe that there is plenty of time to accomplish everything you want to accomplish in your day. Try not to overschedule yourself; instead, leave as much time as possible around the day's main events for unexpected abundance to fill in your schedule.

15

JULY

....

RECEIVER

To be fully present for all the good luck and prosperity coming to you, give yourself permission to be the receiver.

16

JULY

....

ONE A DAY

Send one text, email, or snail mail each day to your brother, sister, parents, a friend, or any other loved one, and tell them how much you appreciate their presence in your life. You can keep your notes short and sweet or make them more elaborate. Notice how more honesty, gratitude, and fulfillment enters your heart and the hearts of others when you do this.

17

JULY
·········

SELF-VALUE

When you take positive action to respect yourself, your self-value becomes your motivating factor. This allows you to feel infinitely good about yourself.

18

JULY
·········

"When riches begin to come they come so quickly, in such great abundance, that one wonders where they have been hiding."

—NAPOLEON HILL

19

JULY

....

YOGA OFF THE MAT

Yoga is more than just a physical practice. Yoga is taking care of yourself, meditating, and so much more. Today, set an intention to be either more aware of your breathing pattern, more attuned to the sounds of nature, or more intuitive about giving yourself kindness and self-care. With your new awareness, let the union between your body, mind, and soul encourage you to practice yoga off the mat.

20

JULY

....

FIELD OF ABUNDANCE

Imagine a field of beautiful flowers bursting with bright colors. In your mind's eye, you are that field of iridescent colors, constantly changing with abundant future prospects.

21

JULY
....

SIMPLE TASK

Pick an easy kitchen chore, like reorganizing the glasses in the cupboard, cleaning the countertops, or cleaning the coffee pot. Let the pride you take in completing these simple tasks continue into your day.

22

JULY
....

UP-TO-DATE THOUGHT

Your negative thoughts are out-of-date and obsolete. Your new expansive thoughts are up-to-date and will continually envelop your positive future.

23

JULY
....

THE ABUNDANT COMPANY YOU KEEP

To further your abundance mindset, surround yourself with other abundance-minded people. Can you think of friends in your circle who upgrade your thinking and creativity and cheer you on? Make a mental list of these close friends to reassure yourself that you are all on abundant, supportive, positive journeys together.

24

JULY
....

FILL YOUR SELF-IMAGE TANK

When you are properly hydrated, your skin looks smoother and more radiant and your inner body functions with ease. Fill up your self-image tank by drinking enough water.

25

DAILY INVENTORY

Make sure you are stocked up with your daily inventory of these attributes:

- Happiness
- Gratitude
- Creativity
- Imagination

Take a moment to close your eyes and visualize how you can infuse them into your day.

26

AFFIRMATION FOR OPPORTUNITY

Remember to always look for silver linings by repeating this affirmation:
"Challenges are opportunities waiting to be turned inside out."

27

....

VALUABLE GIFT

Instead of giving yourself material gifts, give the gift of never-ending time. Make time for the most valuable gift: you.

28

JULY

....

TRUE SELF

There's no need to try to be funnier, be smarter, or make a better first impression. Your true self always shines through flawlessly.

29
JULY
....

180 DEGREES

An example of shifting your scarcity mindset to an abundance mindset is when you shift your ideas, opinions, or stance on something 180 degrees. Can you think of one instance where you have completely changed your mind? Write down how your experience empowered you and gave you ultimate confidence and inner trust.

30
JULY
....

QUARTERBACK

Be the quarterback of your life by calling the plays and being the leader of your own positive thinking and unwavering self-confidence.

31

JULY

·········

HOUR OF POWER

Schedule one hour in your day to do something that you keep putting off. It could be washing the floors, doing the laundry, or taking your recycling to the recycling center. Let this powerful hour of commitment to your goal remind you that completing whatever you set your mind to brings about significant feelings of self-worth.

AUGUST

PERSONAL PROMISES

Write down six promises to yourself. You could promise to always be honest, to always take care of yourself first, to always listen to your gut instincts, or anything else that resonates with you. Carry your personal promises with you today to remind yourself of your unending loyalty to your positive mindset.

2

UTTER RIGHTNESS

Follow the trail that feels the most like ease, happiness, and everything true in your heart.

3

AUGUST

·······

MINDFUL THOUGHTS

These tips will sustain kind and mindful thoughts of abundance:

- Say "thank you" to yourself throughout your day to show self-appreciation.
- Allow vulnerability and humbleness to be your predominant emotions today.

4

AUGUST

·······

BEAUTIFUL PRESENTS

The sunset and sunrise, or a summer rain, are positively awe-inspiring. Let these presents instill everlasting hope and optimism.

5

AUGUST
·········

ARTICULATE AWARENESS

To keep your mind consistently sharp and focused, listen to a symphony orchestra and make a mental note of each instrument that you can hear. Listen for the flute, oboe, clarinet, viola, violin, French horn, or any other instrument you can pick out. Articulate awareness is a precise way to zone in on the present moment.

6

AUGUST
·········

"The test of our progress is not whether we add more to the abundance of those who have much; it is whether we provide enough for those who have too little."

—FRANKLIN D. ROOSEVELT

7

AUGUST

....

GROW FORWARD

Steady, slow, pure, and sweet is your expansive, fulfilling way of growing forward.

8

AUGUST

....

OPPOSITES ATTRACT

The next time you have strong emotions like sadness or worry, think of the opposite emotion instead. If you feel sadness, think of a situation that made you feel exuberantly happy. If you are worried, think of a time in your life when you felt unending joy. Attract the opposite so you can provide your soul with the confidence you need to take charge of your emotions.

9

AUGUST

....

CLOSE YOUR EYES

Close your eyes and look within to see the enormous number of miracles that occur in your world. Seeing these miracles with your imagination will lead you to seeing them as everlasting realities.

10

AUGUST

....

UNIVERSAL SOURCE ENERGY

Sit in a comfortable seated position, breathing naturally. Keeping your eyes open, place your hands in your lap and look at them. In yoga, it is believed that your hands are the link between your energy force and the universe's energy force. As you observe the details of your hands, visualize aligning your sureness and gentleness with the universe as you connect to universal source energy.

11

AUGUST

....

DRAMA-FREE LIFE

Your drama-free life is equally proportional in size, shape, and quality to your massive abundance.

12

AUGUST

....

DAILY DOSE

Remember to always take your daily doses of spiritual medicine:

- Receiving: Receive graciously to build self-worth.
- Positive thinking: Think positively for peace of mind.
- Giving: Give generously for a giving mindset.
- Patience: Practice patience to relieve yourself from unnecessary stress.

13

AUGUST
·········

CONSISTENT VISUALIZING

When you consistently visualize your self-worth and value, you create a guaranteed internal relationship between self-respect and undeniable self-love.

14

AUGUST
·········

AFFIRMATION FOR GOOD FORTUNE

Invite good fortune by reciting this mantra:
  "I am constantly receiving good fortune."

15

AUGUST

....

REST AND RECOVERY

Take 15 minutes to lie on your back with your legs slightly separated and arms comfortably by your sides. Close your eyes and let your breath slow down to your natural relaxation rhythm. Do nothing. Let your nothingness act as an abundant source of rest and recovery.

16

AUGUST

....

SHINING THROUGH

When you get enough sleep and make time to do the things you enjoy, the generous attention you are paying to your inner well-being shines through your ever-glowing face.

17

·········

PASSION, ENERGY, AND ENTHUSIASM

In feng shui, the fire element represents passion, energy, and enthusiasm. To bring more of the eternal fire element into your life, write down the one thing you are most passionate about as well as what gives you the energy and enthusiasm to pursue it.

18

·········

UNLIMITED PEACE

Imagine yourself on a tropical island (real or imagined), with the sun, sea salt, and gentle breezes nourishing your soul with unlimited peace.

19

AUGUST

········

FEEL-GOOD HOUR

Is your favorite time of the day morning, afternoon, or nighttime? Celebrate your feel-good hour by eating a piece of your favorite chocolate or listening or dancing to your favorite song, so that you feel happily invincible.

20

AUGUST

········

WHAT'S WORKING FOR YOU?

Even though change is inevitable, keep the parts of your life that are working for you today. If you like your exercise routine and feel its benefits, stick with it. If you like the connection you feel with your friends when you meet for Sunday brunch, save the date. Keeping the good parts of your routine is a powerful tool for inclusive sureness, steadiness, and solidness.

21
AUGUST
·······

"You see things; and you say 'Why?'
But I dream things that never were;
and I say, 'Why not?'"

—GEORGE BERNARD SHAW

22
AUGUST
·······

EXTREMELY BLESSED LIFE

Today is your day to enjoy your extremely blessed life with grace, poise, and compassion.

23

AUGUST

....

PERMANENT PEACE

Here are a few ways to fill your heart with permanent peace:

- Wake up and listen to the gentle sounds of your inhales and exhales.
- Stop and smell the flowers on your walks.
- Meditate with a soft smile.
- Let the mantra "I am peace" flow steadily through your consciousness.

24

AUGUST

....

EAST, WEST, NORTH, AND SOUTH

From all directions and through all seasons, your dreams and desires are being heard to the edges of the earth.

25

GREATER AND GREATER

Make a list of 10 things that you already have that bring you abundance daily. It could be feeling safe, your home and shelter, your health, or anything you have more than adequate quantities of. When you are grateful for what you have right now, greater and greater abundance will constantly arrive into your life.

26

A NURTURING ENVIRONMENT

A nurturing environment is a non-negotiable factor for creating your loving mindset of abundance.

27

AUGUST
·········

INTERIOR DESIGN YOUR LIFE

To honor yourself as a unique, manifesting being, customize your life plan to your specific needs. If you are feeling bored and uninspired in your work, assess whether you should move on and try something new. If you want to get away from the fast-paced lifestyle and live off the grid, research sustainable-living communities. You are the interior designer of your life, the one who gets to choose all of the color palettes to complete your masterpiece.

28

AUGUST
·········

OPEN TO THE UNIVERSE

Today, commit to being open to the universe and allowing its energy to move through you with your absolute best interest at heart. Your big break is right around the corner.

29
AUGUST
....

MIND–BODY CONNECTION

When you give your mind and body the continuous attention they deserve, they function together seamlessly.

Nourish your body with these potent detoxifying roots:

- Turmeric
- Onion
- Garlic
- Ginger

Nourish your mind with these healthy habits:

- Meditation
- Positive mantras and affirmations
- Vivid imagination
- Receiving and giving gratitude

30

·········

AFFIRMATION OF PATIENCE

It's said that patience achieves more than force. Put this message into action by saying this affirmation:

"My gentle disposition encourages me to be more patient with myself and others."

31

AUGUST

·········

IMPROVISED EXPERIENCES

Your life is a series of experiences. Some outcomes are exactly how you want them to be, and others are less so. Keep forging forward through your improvised experiences, with great purpose and awareness, for a lifetime of abundance.

SEPTEMBER

SEPTEMBER
········

RECHARGE YOUR BATTERIES

Today is your day to recharge your internal batteries. Take a 20-minute rest in the afternoon or right after you get home from work. You can wrap up in a cozy blanket, listen to peaceful music, or spritz your pillow with your favorite scent. Allow your rest to recharge your mind and body through loving self-care.

2

SEPTEMBER
········

BEAUTIFUL LIFE

You have the intelligence and poise to recognize that your thoughts are shaping your abundant lifestyle. Gracefully imagine your beautiful life into existence.

3

SEPTEMBER
....

READ A BOOK

Instead of reaching for the remote, your computer, or your phone, open up a good old-fashioned book. Pick something light and relaxing to read, like a biography, a romance novel, or a humorous fiction book. When you engage with a story other than your own, you give yourself a different outlook and allow your brain to learn and absorb more possibilities for abundant thinking.

4

SEPTEMBER
....

AFFIRMATION FOR CLEAR FOCUS

Clarify your vision with this affirmation:
"I am grateful for my clear focus on what matters most to me."

5

SEPTEMBER
·········

FRIENDLY TIES

Be the friend who watches the neighbor's dog when they are away or the friend who shares ideas about healthy ways to prepare meals. When you are a good friend, it creates a feeling of support and mutual caring that brings long-lasting trust and happiness into your life.

6

SEPTEMBER
·········

SELF-INSPIRED ACTION

Today, turn your great ideas into actions. You could start the juice cleanse you've been thinking about, book that cruise you've been researching, or join the cycling group you've been interested in. Allow your self-inspired action to enrich your life.

7

SEPTEMBER

....

DO IT ANYWAY

When you are unsure about whether you're ready for a big opportunity that has come your way, do it anyway. Put one foot in front of the other, with self-confidence and an ambitious effort.

8

SEPTEMBER

....

THE GIFT OF SELF-APPRECIATION

Today, give yourself the gift of self-appreciation. You could go to your hairdresser and get a new haircut or color, book a staycation at a local B&B, or anything else, as long as it provides abundant gratitude to you.

9

EXPAND YOUR STRENGTHS

Instead of trying to improve on your weaknesses, focus on expanding your strengths. Experience greater abundance through continuous expansiveness.

10

SEPTEMBER
········

"In dreams and in love there are no impossibilities."

—JÁNOS ARANY

11

SEPTEMBER
········

TRANSPORTATION APPRECIATION

Today, when you are driving, taking the subway, or waiting for a cab or the bus, give thanks for the abundance of transportation that you take advantage of every day. Your transportation appreciation will help you get to your dreams and desires in a timely manner.

12

SEPTEMBER
········

REFILL

When you want more self-confidence in your job, your relationship, or your daily life, fill your thoughts with positive affirmations and self-affirming mantras.

13

SEPTEMBER
········

BIG DREAMS

The first step to making your dreams come true is to know what your dreams are. Write down a few of them; the bigger the better! You could sketch your dream villa in Italy, list ideas for your newest invention, or create names for the charitable foundation you've been dreaming about starting. Once you address your big dreams, you begin creating the momentum to achieve them.

14

SEPTEMBER
········

VALUED, HEARD, AND RESPECTED

Birds communicate by calling with chirps, peeps, songs, screeches, or caws. Remember that all living beings, no matter what language they use, are valued, heard, and abundantly respected.

15

GUT INSTINCTS

When you find yourself overthinking a situation, close your eyes and take a few deep breaths. As your breathing slows down, so does your thought pattern. This gives you time to align with your feelings and listen closely to your gut instincts. Fully trust that your intuition is guiding you to the right outcome.

16

SEPTEMBER
....

FOR NOW

Let being true to your heart be more than enough for now.

17

INCLUSIVE MIND-BODY HEALTH

Stretching doesn't just increase flexibility in your body; it also allows your mind to become more pliable and less strict. So make some time to stretch for inclusive mind and body health.

18

INTEGRITY

Today, talk with straightforwardness, truthfulness, and complete honesty. By speaking with integrity and your highest moral quality, you will create more self-value.

19

SEPTEMBER

....

AFFIRMATION FOR DAY AND NIGHT

Remember to practice daily self-kindness with this mantra:
"Every day and every night, I generously give myself loving encouragement."

20

SEPTEMBER

....

HIGHER HEIGHTS

Ensure that your amazing, creative ideas are growing through your consistent dedication to appreciating yourself, trusting yourself, and self-confidence.

21
SEPTEMBER
·········

LIFE MAP

When you don't get the promotion, your audition doesn't go well, or you get a flat tire, imagine that these setbacks saved you from moving backward. In fact, imagine that they moved you forward in an unseen, vibrational way. Can you think of an instance when a situation seemed like a depressing setback at first, but because of it, your life changed for the better? Remember that moment, and realize that your life map is always moving you forward.

22
SEPTEMBER
·········

POWERFUL TOOL

Take five slow, deep inhales and exhales to ground yourself in the present moment. You will be delightfully surprised by how a few deep breaths can be a powerful tool for centering your mental and physical state.

23

SEPTEMBER

....

FAREWELL

Say farewell to self-doubt and say hello to abundant trust in yourself, from the tips of your toes to the crown of your head.

24

SEPTEMBER

....

THIRD-EYE CENTER

As you sit comfortably with your eyes closed, cup your hands over your closed eyes and imagine a soft light in between your eyebrows, at your third eye. Your third-eye center is said to be the place where intuition, imagination, and insight live. Quietly observe the soft light and sensations of your meditation, without judgment or fear.

25

SEPTEMBER

....

TREASURE CHEST

All of the coins, gold, or silver you could acquire in your life will never match the never-ending concentration of wealth found within your soul.

26

SEPTEMBER

....

EARTH LOVER

To become closer to Mother Nature, try these earth-loving practices:

1. Drink herbal teas that are free of preservatives.
2. Keep a supply of stones and crystals on hand.
3. Touch the earth with your feet or body each day.
4. Introduce more raw foods into your diet.

27

SEPTEMBER

....

MINDFUL LISTENING

The next time you are with a coworker, a family member, or a friend, don't just hear their words—really listen to what they are saying. Mindful listening is an act of loving-kindness. Feel how deeply people appreciate it when you truly listen to them.

28

SEPTEMBER

....

STABILITY AND CONFIDENCE

A yoga practice is an anchor that prevents you from drifting and brings you back to your intended direction. Let yoga be the anchor that provides stability and confidence to your life.

29

SEPTEMBER
. . . .

"Many eyes go through the meadow, but few see the flowers."

—RALPH WALDO EMERSON

30

SEPTEMBER
. . . .

SPEEDY RESULTS

You are forever progressing past your wildest imagination of what success means. An open mind and open heart invite speedy results.

OCTOBER

1

OCTOBER
. . . .

LIFE'S MASTERPIECE

Once you have discovered your passion, ward off unnecessary distractions until all that is left is your life's masterpiece.

2

OCTOBER
. . . .

TRANQUIL ESCAPE

Close your eyes and visualize a charming, overflowing garden filled with lovely, colorful flowers, bridges arching over swan-filled lakes, and manicured rose and lavender bushes. Allow your visualization to bring a tranquil escape from your busy day-to-day life.

3

OCTOBER

....

20/20 VISION

When you look through the kaleidoscope of colors, patterns, and reflections of your life, remember that the sharpness of your vision is uniquely tied to what you choose to see.

4

OCTOBER

....

LEAN INTO YOUR ABUNDANCE

Lean into your abundance with these self-confident affirmations:

1. I am worthy.
2. I am in the right place at the right time.
3. I am in my element.
4. I am ready.

5

OCTOBER

. . . .

ONE-WAY TICKET

You are boarding your life experiences on a one-way ticket to everlasting happiness.

6

OCTOBER

. . . .

PREPAREDNESS

If you want to live in the South of France, prepare by taking French lessons. If you want to start a foundation to save homeless dogs, prepare by working at an animal shelter. Welcome greatness through preparedness.

7

OCTOBER

·········

"Life is to be fortified by many friendships.
To love, and to be loved, is the greatest
happiness of existence."

—SYDNEY SMITH

8

OCTOBER

·········

REPETITION, REPETITION, REPETITION

When you focus your mind on abundance for one day, you receive one day of
abundance. Through daily repetition of your abundance mindset, you receive
timeless abundance.

9

OCTOBER
·········

SOULFUL AWARENESS

Close your eyes and let your emotions be raw and honest to fully feel your soulful awareness. Openhearted sensations of happiness, gratitude, and complete humility work together for your greater good.

10

OCTOBER
·········

PRIVILEGE

You have been given the infinite privilege of choosing your destiny through your daily thoughts and mindset.

11

OCTOBER

....

YOU ARE LOVED

Always remember, without question, that you are loved on your life's journey. Friends, family, spiritual teachers, and counselors are readily available to you. Reach out to your trusted source of family, community, or professional help whenever you feel like you need some extra guidance and unconditional love.

12

OCTOBER

....

DAYDREAMER

Allow your mind to occasionally wander in a dreamlike state during waking hours. Enjoy the sheer pleasure and ultimate freedom of daydreaming.

13

OCTOBER

....

UNDERSTANDING YOUR GOALS

Check in about your personal reasons for desiring a specific goal by asking yourself these three questions:

1. Will I feel more abundant or more depleted after achieving my goal?
2. What is my motivation for my goal?
3. Am I ready and abundantly willing to take the appropriate action to achieve my goal?

14

OCTOBER

....

AFFIRMATION FOR WISHING

Bring to mind a dream you have for your future. Now close your eyes and repeat this affirmation to help manifest your wishes:

"As I toss my coin into the wishing well, I visualize my wish coming true."

15

SUBTLE SHIFT

Sit comfortably, with your eyes closed and your palms open on your knees. Inhale slowly through your nose, and exhale slowly through your mouth, blowing all of the air out of your lungs. Continue this breathing pattern for five minutes. You will experience a subtle shift to calming relaxation.

16

OCTOBER
....

CREATOR OF YOUR WORLD

The universe applauds you for having the courage and compassion to be the abundant creator of your world.

17
OCTOBER
·········

POSITIVE ENERGY FIELD

Improve your positive energy field by making a list of five things that make you happy and feel good. It could be watching a funny movie, taking a bubble bath, or going for a walk with your dog. You are benefiting from continuous happiness on a deep, cellular level.

18
OCTOBER
·········

HASHTAG TODAY

Today, declare that your dominant mindset is one of outstanding possibilities and opportunities. #Today is your day of great abundance.

19

OCTOBER

....

HEALING PRACTICE

Lie on your back with eyes closed and a pillow behind your head. Rest your arms by your sides. Mentally scan your body, starting at your toes and moving all the way up to the crown of your head. Notice if you have sore muscles, tight hips, or any other tension in your body. If you find that any area is tense, take a deep breath into that area and visualize all stress or tightness dissipating. Use your breath as an overall healing practice for well-being.

20

OCTOBER

....

YOUR OWN WAY OF THINKING

Your own organic way of thinking serves your best interests far better than conventional thinking.

21

OCTOBER
....

AFFIRM AND REAFFIRM

Thinking positive thoughts, reading affirmations, and repeating daily mantras is the path to abundance. Wake up visualizing the beautiful day ahead, stick inspiring mantras on your bathroom mirror or use any other method you like. Affirm and reaffirm positivity throughout your day to dispel any insecurity or doubt.

22

OCTOBER
....

"People become really quite remarkable when they start thinking that they can do things. When they believe in themselves, they have the first secret of success."

—NORMAN VINCENT PEALE

23

BACK TO THE BASICS

The foundation of your right choice, right speech, right etiquette, right thought, and right success can be found each day when you acknowledge and return to the basics.

24

OCTOBER
·········

QUIET INTERVALS

Several times throughout your day, close your eyes and sit quietly for one minute to clear and quiet your mind. Use these quiet intervals as a way to keep yourself balanced and laser-focused on the clear intention of manifesting abundance.

25
OCTOBER

EMOTIONAL CHOICE

Every day is a new day to choose gratitude. Make a personal commitment to making appreciation and gratitude your emotional choice.

26
OCTOBER

BLISSFUL, FEEL-GOOD DAY

Make sure that you're stocked up on your favorite self-care products to help you feel good about yourself and give you confidence. Your face cream, body oil, bath salts, and hair masks all bring you self-worth and self-confidence for a nourishing, blissful, feel-good day.

27

OCTOBER
....

FIRST PLACE

Today, your first-place trophy is awarded to you for your consistency, determination, and complete commitment to your health, well-being, and overall healthy mindset.

28

OCTOBER
....

DESIRES AND DREAMS

Let your heart guide you to your greatest desires and dreams, from love to lifestyle to wealth. Through meditation, positive visualization, and absolute devotion and faith, you will receive what your heart wants and so much more.

29
OCTOBER
········

HOMEMADE AND HUMBLED

Have you ever walked into a house and immediately smelled cookies coming out of the oven or fresh bread baking? Close your eyes and evoke these welcoming, homemade scents to remind yourself how these nurturing pleasures make you feel grateful, humbled, and taken care of.

30
OCTOBER
········

AFFIRMATION FOR COMPASSION

Reaffirm your compassionate mindset with this mantra:

"My unbending compassion for myself, my work, and my family is consistently thriving."

31

OCTOBER

....

NO TIME LIKE THE PRESENT

It is always the present moment that brings you back to your greatest awareness of self-worth. Now is the time to adorn yourself with self-esteem, self-respect, and self-value.

NOVEMBER

1
NOVEMBER
....

GRACE AND COMPASSION

You receive endless, loving, supportive vibrational energy each day through grace and compassion.

2
NOVEMBER
....

EFFORTLESS FLOW

Trust that the universe is scheduling your day, your week, and your year and is dedicated to synchronizing with the best possible outcome. Your job today is to plan the best you can, then let go of being attached to your schedule. Your workout time could be moved up an hour, your dinner plans could get canceled, or your bedtime could arrive earlier. When you let go of specific outcomes, your life flows effortlessly.

3
NOVEMBER
....

"I wish you all the joy that you can wish."

—WILLIAM SHAKESPEARE

4
NOVEMBER
....

WORDS HAVE POWER

You have the power to transform your mood and the mood of others around you through the words you use. Here is your checklist of words to use today:

1. Words that are gracious
2. Words that are thankful
3. Words that are nourishing
4. Words that are honest and open

5

NOVEMBER

· · · · · · · ·

SWAP IMPATIENCE FOR PATIENCE

Your abundance mindset is teaching you that everything you desire is arriving when it is supposed to. Dig deep in your soul and swap out your impatience for patience.

6

NOVEMBER

· · · · · · · ·

POOL OF ABUNDANCE

Become a beginner student of something that you have never learned about before. You could sign up for a foreign-language class, take piano lessons, or subscribe to an online mentoring group. When you expand your knowledge, you expand your pool of abundance.

7

NOVEMBER
·········

THE PATH OF LEAST RESISTANCE

The path of least resistance is a path of forward motion, fueled by your mindset that all things great and small are possible.

8

NOVEMBER
·········

COLLECTIVE GRATITUDE

What you think and feel, you pass on to others around you. Today, set your emotions and thoughts to constant gratitude, and witness the ripple effect of collective gratitude that they create.

9

SEASONAL ABUNDANCE

Your abundant mindset of joy and happiness flows with ease in spring, summer, fall, and winter.

10

NOVEMBER
·······

MINDFUL WALKING MEDITATION

Take long, slow, deep breaths in and out through the nose as you walk at a moderate pace. Comfortably extend your inhalations and exhalations as you walk. Your awareness of your breath, combined with active walking, delivers abundant well-being to your mind, body, and soul as you engage in mindful walking meditation.

11

NOVEMBER

· · · · · · · ·

GENTLENESS OVER HARSHNESS

Deciding to practice gentleness instead of harshness doesn't just apply to how you treat other people; it also extends to how you treat yourself.

12

NOVEMBER

· · · · · · · ·

CONVERSATION PEACE

Encourage your inner voice to be calm and peaceful. You could say to yourself, "I am calm and balanced today," "I am holding space for a peaceful mindset," or "I feel relaxed." Peaceful conversation is your dialogue of immeasurable calm, harmony, and joy.

13

NOVEMBER
....

AFFIRMATION FOR PERSEVERANCE

Foster steadfast patience with this mantra:

"I am certain that my steady, positive attitude is leading me with perseverance toward my goals."

14

NOVEMBER
....

ENERGETIC BEAUTY

Uncover fresh, clean, vibrant energy in your house through cleaning. Remove dead flowers or dried plants, dust off furniture, and remove cobwebs. Cleaning removes stale energy to expose energetic beauty.

15

NOVEMBER

········

DON'T OVERTHINK IT

When you ruminate about the past and worry about the future, your brain is working overtime on things it cannot change. Don't overthink it; experience the bounty of what is.

16

NOVEMBER

········

RELAXED IN ACTION

Most professional athletes—from runners to gymnasts to basketball players—perform best when they are at their most relaxed. Think of a time you played on a sports team, a recent workout, or a yoga class—the important thing is to recall a moment where you were completely relaxed in action. By not forcing the outcome, you become vibrationally aligned with your mind and body.

17

NOVEMBER
·········

CALL IT TO YOU

Feel your abundance, see your abundance, and visualize your abundance. You are preparing for the enormous amounts of prosperity, wealth, and health that you are calling to you.

18

NOVEMBER
·········

GRATITUDE ATTENTION

Write down at least three spiritual characteristics you have, like joy, wisdom, happiness, intuitiveness, or any others you can think of. Write a sentence or two about the significance of each one, and give thanks and appreciation for it. As you give gratitude for your spiritual richness, the universe provides in magical ways.

19

NOVEMBER

....

DIVINE LOVE

You are a tripod of immeasurable compassion, trustworthiness, and balance. Stand strong and tall on your foundation of divine love.

20

NOVEMBER

....

MOTHER NATURE'S SANCTUARY

To create or increase your feeling of connection to nature, touch the freshly fallen snow, climb to the top of a mountain, walk through a forest or jungle, or swim in the ocean. The simplicity and complexity of Mother Nature's sanctuary helps you experience inspired acceptance on a higher level.

21

NOVEMBER
. . . .

"Meditation is nourishing and blossoming the divine within you."

—AMIT RAY

22

NOVEMBER
. . . .

FORECAST

The sun doesn't shine its brilliance every day, nor do storm clouds roll in daily. Stay steadfast in your abundant mindset, no matter what the weather forecast is.

23

NOVEMBER

·······

STATE-OF-THE-ART THINKING

Make a mental list of the ways you are motivated to update your way of thinking. You could break old thinking patterns, look at a challenge with a different
perspective, make new acquaintances, or take any other step to see things with
a fresh outlook. When you get in the habit of state-of-the-art thinking, your
creativity starts to overflow.

24

NOVEMBER

·······

GENEROUSLY WITHIN YOUR MEANS

You can live generously within your means and also share with others. In yoga,
this is called *aparigraha*.

25

NOVEMBER
....

RESTORE YOURSELF

There is a mental correspondence for every disease. Today, restore yourself back to health by allowing healing thoughts as your body follows the natural process of repairing itself.

26

NOVEMBER
....

NEVER TOO LATE

When you think you are too old to go back to school, missed your chance at love, or are too fearful to start a new career, remember that it is never too late. The infinite spirit is always full of sureness and willing and ready to support you.

27

LISTEN TO THIS

As you are making your morning coffee, mowing the lawn, walking your dog, or engaging in any other routine activity, listen to a favorite, calming song on your headphones. Let the music evoke happiness, ease, and a peaceful state of being. Take this feeling with you throughout your day.

28

NOVEMBER
....

AFFIRMATION OF ENDLESS GOOD

Bring goodness into your life by saying this affirmation whenever you need to:
"I receive endless good, in endless ways, in endless places."

29

NOVEMBER
....

INFINITE INTELLIGENCE

Meditate on your dreams every day with great loyalty to connect to your infinite intelligence through your subconscious mind.

30

NOVEMBER
....

SELF-EXPRESSION

Boldly trust the self-expression of your feelings and opinions. You mold the shape of your abundant lifestyle.

DECEMBER

1

DECEMBER

....

WEATHER VIBES

Let the sun shower cheerfulness and brightness on you. Let the snowfall bring peace and beauty. Let the rain fall down from the sky and wash away your worries. Give thanks to the many ways the weather is always supporting your abundance mindset.

2

DECEMBER

....

AURA OF PROTECTION

You are forever watched over and taken care of by a gentle aura of protection.

3

DECEMBER
....

GOOD-WORD JOURNEY

Use your words as confident instruments to endlessly spread positivity to yourself and others. In your mind, make a list of supporting words you can use throughout your day to encourage yourself and those around you. You could use *yes, mindful, gratitude, progress, giving, clearheadedness, all-encompassing,* or any other words that benefit your good-word journey.

4

DECEMBER
....

COMFORT AND EASE

When you make decisions based on honesty and self-trust, your heart floods with comfort and ease.

5

DECEMBER

....

SUNSET

Go outside during the sunset. If you are in cold weather, bundle up. Watch the sunset and take a few deep, calming breaths. Congratulate yourself on the completion of your day. Respect and honor the daily cycle of life through humbled eyes of gratitude.

6

DECEMBER

....

"I challenge you to make your life a masterpiece. I challenge you to join the ranks of those people who live what they teach, who walk their talk."

—TONY ROBBINS

7

DECEMBER

········

CULTIVATING ENERGY

By constantly implementing abundance in your life, you are cultivating the energy of self-realization and ever-growing self-esteem.

8

DECEMBER

········

ORGANICALLY SOURCED

Find your inspiration through your own unique experiences. Organically source what nourishes you through laughter, feeds your soul with happiness, and quenches your thirst for knowledge. When you pay attention to what inspires you, it leads you to opportunities that are meaningful and unique to you.

9

DECEMBER
....

NO COMPETITION

What is yours is given to you through your unwavering mindset of abundance. What is given to others is theirs through the universe's unwavering abundance. There is no competition or shortage of abundance.

10

DECEMBER
....

WIDE AWAKE

Today, practice being completely wide awake to your aspirations as you repeat these mantras:

1. My good always comes to me.
2. I have endless opportunities.
3. My mind and body are in sync.
4. I clearly hear my voice and trust my intuition.

11

DECEMBER
·······

LITTLE BY LITTLE

Your life is not a race to the finish line. Instead, it is a progression of experiences that lead you to your ultimate destination and beyond. Little by little, you create your own beautiful, full life.

12

DECEMBER
·······

SELF-LOVE DAY

Design a self-love day with the intention of taking extra care of yourself through loving acts of kindness. You could make fresh-squeezed orange juice for yourself, book a massage or facial, or just stay in bed reading a book. Give yourself gentle, loving attention to remind yourself how abundant you are.

13

DECEMBER
....

AFFIRMATION FOR SHARING

Release yourself from greed by reciting this affirmation:

   "I am a sharing and caring being that doesn't hoard wealth, health, or prosperity."

14

DECEMBER
....

RADIANCE

The light, love, and radiance you exude comes from your deep connection to your abundantly manifested core spirit.

15

········

REST DAY

Today, rejuvenate yourself by lying down in your bed, sitting at the park, lying under an umbrella at the beach, or any way you can comfortably rest your mind and body. Think of why it is important to rest and what your rest day accomplishes. It could be nurturing self-love in your heart center, refreshing creativity in your thoughts, or healing sensations in your body. Acknowledge your complete self-worth through your rest day.

16

DECEMBER

········

IN DUE TIME

Don't focus on the urgency you feel in obtaining your goal. Do your work, keep your values, accept change along the way, and the perfect outcome will come in due time.

17

DECEMBER
·········

PEAKS AND VALLEYS

Focus on a single topic that signifies a successful life to you in this moment. It could be a great professional career, a solid marriage, achieving your target weight, or any other goal that resonates with you today. Accept the peaks and valleys that will occur on your journey with self-compassion as you observe your achievements coming to fruition.

18

DECEMBER
·········

SPIRITUAL CURRENCY

Wholeheartedly believe in yourself with fervor and passion, as you are your own spiritual currency.

19
DECEMBER
·······

VINYASA FLOW

When your breath connects with your movement in a smooth, flowy pattern, you are practicing vinyasa flow yoga. Take a vinyasa flow walk: imagine your steps, your breath, your ease of pace, and your inner and outer awareness seamlessly moving together, creating a peaceful state of being.

20
DECEMBER
·······

SELF-REFLECT

Let your inner communication with yourself be filled with appreciation and love as you self-reflect with contentment.

21
DECEMBER
....

SELF-COURAGE

Do you have the courage to let your walls down and unguard your heart? Today, instead of hiding or repressing your feelings, take a risk and tell someone special how you honestly feel. Let the process of taking a heartfelt risk be the way to self-courage.

22
DECEMBER
....

"Beauty is eternity gazing at itself
in a mirror. But you are eternity
and you are the mirror."

—KHALIL GIBRAN

23
DECEMBER
....

FLEXIBLE OUTLOOK

When you have a flexible outlook, you become less stressed and more harmonious with your decision-making.

24
DECEMBER
....

EVENNESS

Your calm disposition leans toward a tranquil evenness, which suits your continual balance of emotions.

25
DECEMBER
....

STEADY DISCIPLINE

Sit quietly on two pillows or stacked blankets, with eyes closed and hands in your lap. Relax your hips and knees, and inhale and exhale slowly through the nose, breathing in for six counts and out for six counts. For five minutes, focus your mind on your count, as distractions, sounds, and thoughts fade away. Your steady discipline fills your mind, body, and soul with abundant serenity.

26
DECEMBER
....

ALL THE TIME

Your true nature is a feeling of never wanting anything, because you have more than enough of everything all the time.

27

DECEMBER

....

VISUAL RISK

Without boundaries or limits, take a visual risk and dream far beyond what you think is possible. Only then will you scratch the surface of your incoming abundance.

28

DECEMBER

....

A PICTURE IS WORTH A THOUSAND WORDS

Viewing a photo's essence in contemplative silence tells us more than any verbal description can. Rather than considering your thoughts through an internal dialogue, silently observe your life in your mind's eye to gain a broader, abundance-based perspective.

29

DECEMBER

....

LIFE OF A GIVER

Make a list of generous acts you regularly perform that increase your happiness, connect you with your life's purpose, and bring you fulfillment. It could be as simple as making dinner for your parents once a week, giving to a local charity, or volunteering at your kid's school. Continually lead the life of a giver, for greater purpose and spiritual connectedness.

30

DECEMBER

....

AFFIRMATION FOR STEPPING INTO ENERGY

Confidently step into your abundance with this affirmation:

"As I step into my energy of abundance, I create and receive more and more each day."

31

DECEMBER
·········

CONTINUE YOUR JOURNEY

You have the tools, the skills, the knowledge, and the sensitivity for a beautiful life. Give yourself this mantra to continue your journey:

"I practice self-love and gratitude daily to expand my abundant mindset."

Resources

BOOKS

- *As a Man Thinketh* by James Allen
- *Ask and It Is Given: Learning to Manifest Your Desires* by Esther and Jerry Hicks
- *The Complete Works of Florence Scovel Shinn* by Florence Scovel Shinn
- *What I Know for Sure* by Oprah Winfrey
- *A Year of Meditation: Daily Moments of Peace, Joy, and Calm* by Nora Day

WEBSITES

- NoraDayLive.com: My site offers yoga, meditation, lifestyle blogs, plant-based recipes, and all things abundant.
- Gaia.com: A large collection of videos for expanding your consciousness.

APPS

- EnVision: Your Vision Board: For 10 minutes a day, focus on what's important, prepare for life's big events, and show up as the best version of yourself when it counts.

- **Louise Hay Affirmation Meditations: Essential Affirmations for Health, Love, Success & Self-Esteem:** Louise L. Hay's app uses 16 of her most effective "Power Thoughts," delivered using a whole-body learning process, from stunningly beautiful, animated meditation exercises to cutting-edge audio brainwave technology.
- **Mantra: Daily Affirmations:** Unique affirmations for every day that can be personalized with background sounds, colors, and fonts.

PODCASTS

- **The Abundance Project:** Derek Rydall reveals his time-tested system for activating the "Abundance Principle," where you will discover how to generate real-world abundance in every area of your life.
- **Having It ALL: Conversations about Living an Abundant Loving Life:** Matthew Bivens shares belief systems, tools, and support systems to design your best life and live your full potential.
- **Into Abundance:** Regan Hillyer brings powerful ideas, concepts, wisdoms, and inspirations to receive abundance and prosperity in all aspects of your life.
- **The Mindset Mentor:** Rob Dial challenges his audience to live a life of love and purpose.
- **The Tony Robbins Podcast:** Tony Robbins shares proven strategies and tactics so you can achieve results in business, relationships, health, and finances.

Acknowledgments

Thank you to everyone who strives to live a beautiful, abundant life through gratitude, kindness, and love. You all make this world a peaceful planet of forever abundance.

To all the yoga teachers, spiritual leaders, and mentors I've had the opportunity to study under, I want to thank you for being a tremendous inspiration.

To everyone at Callisto Media, your constant support and encouragement for my books has been truly heartwarming. I feel the love! Special thanks to Adrian Potts, my kind editor, for trusting and inspiring me.

Lastly, I want to thank Mother Maui for your brilliant colors, healing ocean swims, beach walks in paradise, and overwhelming abundance for supporting me through writing this book. Mahalo.

About the Author

 **Nora Day,** the author of *A Year of Meditation*, is a leading voice and inspirational speaker for all things meditation, yoga, and living an abundant lifestyle. Nora is 500 E-RYT Yoga Alliance certified and the founder of Yoginora.com, a one-stop shop for yoga, meditation, plant-based recipes, and abundant lifestyle choices. Nora's approach to yoga, meditation, and abundant living is very reflective of her Midwest upbringing. She's dedicated to keeping it simple and honest, without fluff or fakeness. Nora embodies what she teaches, combining yoga, meditation, diet, and a peaceful, abundant lifestyle in her formula for health and happiness.

CPSIA information can be obtained
at www.ICGtesting.com
Printed in the USA
JSHW041344180723
44883JS00003B/15

9 781648 767814